THE ULTIMATE

travel

PLANNER + JOURNAL

crafted
travel company

Published by Crafted Travel Company
2 Via Silla
Rancho Santa Margarita, CA 92688
www.craftedtravelco.com

ISBN:
978-1-7373535-6-0

"We travel not to escape life, but for life not to escape us."

- ANONYMOUS

Created by travel professionals to help you plan and organize your upcoming vacation. We didn't stop there, however. We've also included journal and memory pages so you can write and keep momentos from your vacation. In the end you'll have a beautiful permanent keepsake of your journey.

If you need assistance at any point in planning your vacation, please feel free to contact us at hello@craftedtravelco.com or www.craftedtravelco.com. We would be happy to help in any way!

Bon Voyage!

Crafted Travel Company

CONTENTS

Passenger + Emergency Information

passenger
information

EMERGENCY CONTACT AT HOME:

TRAVEL INSURANCE/TRAVEL EMERGENCY PHONE + POLICY NUMBER:

PASSENGER 1 (FULL NAME AS SPELLED ON PASSPORT OR ID)

PASSPORT NUMBER, EXPIRATION, + ISSUE DATE:

TSA PRECHECK OR GLOBAL ENTRY NUMBER:

AIRLINE MEMBERSHIP NUMBER:

NOTES (HEALTH/MEDICAL ALERT/PREFERENCES)

PASSENGER 2 (FULL NAME AS SPELLED ON PASSPORT OR ID)

PASSPORT NUMBER, EXPIRATION, + ISSUE DATE:

TSA PRECHECK OR GLOBAL ENTRY NUMBER:

AIRLINE MEMBERSHIP NUMBER:

NOTES (HEALTH/MEDICAL ALERT/PREFERENCES)

passenger information

PASSENGER 3 (FULL NAME AS SPELLED ON PASSPORT OR ID)

PASSPORT NUMBER, EXPIRATION, + ISSUE DATE:

TSA PRECHECK OR GLOBAL ENTRY NUMBER:

AIRLINE MEMBERSHIP NUMBER:

NOTES (HEALTH/MEDICAL ALERT/PREFERENCES)

PASSENGER 4 (FULL NAME AS SPELLED ON PASSPORT OR ID)

PASSPORT NUMBER, EXPIRATION, + ISSUE DATE:

TSA PRECHECK OR GLOBAL ENTRY NUMBER:

AIRLINE MEMBERSHIP NUMBER:

NOTES (HEALTH/MEDICAL ALERT/PREFERENCES)

PASSENGER 5 (FULL NAME AS SPELLED ON PASSPORT OR ID)

PASSPORT NUMBER, EXPIRATION, + ISSUE DATE:

TSA PRECHECK OR GLOBAL ENTRY NUMBER:

AIRLINE MEMBERSHIP NUMBER:

NOTES (HEALTH/MEDICAL ALERT/PREFERENCES)

passenger information

PASSENGER 6 (FULL NAME AS SPELLED ON PASSPORT OR ID)

PASSPORT NUMBER, EXPIRATION, + ISSUE DATE:

TSA PRECHECK OR GLOBAL ENTRY NUMBER:

AIRLINE MEMBERSHIP NUMBER:

NOTES (HEALTH/MEDICAL ALERT/PREFERENCES)

PASSENGER 7 (FULL NAME AS SPELLED ON PASSPORT OR ID)

PASSPORT NUMBER, EXPIRATION, + ISSUE DATE:

TSA PRECHECK OR GLOBAL ENTRY NUMBER:

AIRLINE MEMBERSHIP NUMBER:

NOTES (HEALTH/MEDICAL ALERT/PREFERENCES)

PASSENGER 8 (FULL NAME AS SPELLED ON PASSPORT OR ID)

PASSPORT NUMBER, EXPIRATION, + ISSUE DATE:

TSA PRECHECK OR GLOBAL ENTRY NUMBER:

AIRLINE MEMBERSHIP NUMBER:

NOTES (HEALTH/MEDICAL ALERT/PREFERENCES)

Vacation Planning

Researching your destination

Discover new destination ideas or take a deeper dive into your preferred destination with the following resources. These are the links our professional travel advisors use most often when planning a new vacation for a client.

When choosing your next destination, here are the top 4 steps to take:

1. **Choose your budget** - Not only what you want to spend in total for your trip, but also break it down to the max you would like to spend on flights (or traveling to your destination), lodging, activities, food, and shopping (or extras you might spend money on). Knowing this at the beginning will help guide your decisions going forward.See budget worksheets on page below.
2. **Get Inspired** - Visit Google Flights (https://www.google.com/travel/flights) and scroll down to the *Explore Destinations* map. This handy tool will allow you to search the entire world based on when you go, how long you want to stay, and how much you want to spend.
3. **Research Top Choices on YouTube** - Once you have a few top ideas, research them on YouTube and TripAdvisor to help narrow down your choice further.
4. **Choose when to go** - The number one way to save money on travel is to stay flexible on dates. Use tools such as the Google *Explore Destinations* we mentioned above or *Hopper* (phone app available on Apple and Android) to find the best time to go that will save you the most money. Another great resource for this is at https://championtraveler.com/best-time-to-travel/. This website shares a ton of data on weather, crowds, and overall experience in various months.

For **detailed walk-throughs of how to plan your vacation**, be sure to visit our YouTube channel using the QR Code below:

Our favorite research sites:

- **Google Flights Explore Destinations** - excellent place to get inspiration for your next vacation
- **YouTube** - fantastic for personal experiences and videos of the destination and/or activity you are seeking. Also has good information on safety concerns, destination nuances and tricks, and so much more.
- **Google** - always a good place to start for general articles and ideas.
- **TripAdvisor** - we use this mostly after we've chosen a destination, but it can be used to help you choose as well. Search potential cities to see personal reviews of the area, hotels, and what there is to do.

trip research

potential destinations

BEST DATES TO GO:

potential destinations

WHERE CAN WE GO? AND BY WHAT ROUTE (FLY, DRIVE,
CRUISE, TRAIN, ETC)

BEST DATES TO GO:

potential lodging

WHAT ARE OUR OPTIONS?

activities

WHAT ARE THE TOP ACTIVITIES WE'D LIKE TO EXPERIENCE?

restaurants/pubs

WHAT RESTAURANTS WOULD YOU LIKE TO GO TO?

other elements

IS THERE ANYTHING ELSE YOU'D LIKE TO SEE, DO, OR EXPLORE?

Research Travel Requirements

As you start thinking about your upcoming vacation, one of the first things you need to research is travel restrictions. Unfortunately, the pandemic has forever changed the way we travel so it's something we will always need to be aware of.

This is of particular importance if you are traveling in 2021-2022.

Here are the top resources for discovering what you will need for your vacation:

If traveling to Europe:
The first resource to visit is ReOpen EU. This website and app were created by the European Travel Authority as a resource for anyone needing to travel to or through the EU. This only applies to countries in the European Union, however, so if you are traveling to the UK, for instance, their information would not be here.

ReOpen EU - https://reopen.europa.eu/en

From the ReOpen EU site, click the Travel Plan button, then select your starting country and destination from the drop-down menu.

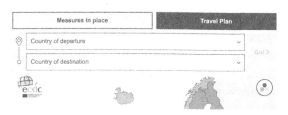

This will bring you to a summary of the items needed to enter that country. This will include helpful links if you need to research further.

31

If you would like to research a little deeper, click on the links they supply on this page.

For everywhere else:

For more information, you can also Google your **destination + travel requirements** to see the latest articles and details.

Our favorite places to check are the *destination's Tourism Board, State Department, or Embassy.* Additionally, your airline may have details on international travel that may help. For instance, Delta Airlines has details regarding travel to Italy due to their recent COVID-Tested Flights.

As you conduct this research, be sure to check for the following:

If vaccinated
- Documentation requirements
- Is testing also required?
- Are there any quarantine or self-isolation requirements?
- Does your vaccine need to be uploaded anywhere (for instance an app or verification program)?
- What is the minimum age that would need this?

If non-vaccinated
- What type of test is required (PCR/NAAT, Antigen, etc.)?
- What timeframe does it need to be taken within?
- If you've recovered from COVID, will they take a certification? If so, for what timeframe?
- What is the minimum age that would need this?

For all of the above, check what else is needed, such as:
- Passenger Locator Forms
- Health Declarations
- Safe Travels Program Registration
- National App or Program Registration
- Travel Insurance
- Or anything else aside from vaccination and negative testing proof

IMPORTANT NOTE

Be sure to *continue to check travel requirements after you've booked your trip and DURING your trip*. This is particularly important if you are visiting multiple cities or countries.

Travel requirements can **change almost daily**, so you need to stay on top of any new developments. Clients of our have had plans change on them while on vacation, so it's important to always know what you are in for as you travel between the different countries or cities.

This is **also important for your return home.** For instance, as of this writing, in the US you need a negative COVID test within 72 hours of your return from another country. This may change at any time so be sure to stay on top of this information as well using the QR Code below (US State Department link)

travel requirements

WHAT COUNTRY(IES) ARE YOU VISITNG?

WHAT COUNTRY(IES) ARE YOU TRANSITING THROUGH (EVEN TO JUST CHANGE PLANES)?

IS ANYONE IN YOUR PARTY VACCINATED? WHICH VACCIINE?

OF THOSE NOT VACCINATED, HAVE THEY RECOVERED WITHIN LAST 6 MOS (CAN THEY GET A CERTIFICATE PROVING SUCH)?

travel requirements

COUNTRY:

TAKE VACCINES? WHICH ONES? WHAT DO YOU NEED TO SHOW
TO PROVE VACCINATION?

DO YOU NEED A NEGATIVE TEST? WHAT KIND (PCR, ANTIGEN,
ETC)? WITHIN WHAT TIME FRAME OF ARRIVAL? DO YOU HAVE
TO RE-TEST AT CERTAIN INTERVAL

WILL THEY TAKE RECOVERY CERTIFICATES? WITHIN WHAT TIME
FRAME OF ARRIVAL?

WHAT ELSE IS REQUIRED (PASSENGER LOCATOR FORMS,
REGISTRATIONS, TRAVEL INSURANCE, APPS, DECLARATION
FORMS, ETC)?

travel requirements

COUNTRY:

TAKE VACCINES? WHICH ONES? WHAT DO YOU NEED TO SHOW
TO PROVE VACCINATION?

DO YOU NEED A NEGATIVE TEST? WHAT KIND (PCR, ANTIGEN,
ETC)? WITHIN WHAT TIME FRAME OF ARRIVAL? DO YOU HAVE
TO RE-TEST AT CERTAIN INTERVAL

WILL THEY TAKE RECOVERY CERTIFICATES? WITHIN WHAT TIME
FRAME OF ARRIVAL?

WHAT ELSE IS REQUIRED (PASSENGER LOCATOR FORMS,
REGISTRATIONS, TRAVEL INSURANCE, APPS, DECLARATION
FORMS, ETC)?

travel requirements

COUNTRY:

TAKE VACCINES? WHICH ONES? WHAT DO YOU NEED TO SHOW TO PROVE VACCINATION?

DO YOU NEED A NEGATIVE TEST? WHAT KIND (PCR, ANTIGEN, ETC)? WITHIN WHAT TIME FRAME OF ARRIVAL? DO YOU HAVE TO RE-TEST AT CERTAIN INTERVAL

WILL THEY TAKE RECOVERY CERTIFICATES? WITHIN WHAT TIME FRAME OF ARRIVAL?

WHAT ELSE IS REQUIRED (PASSENGER LOCATOR FORMS, REGISTRATIONS, TRAVEL INSURANCE, APPS, DECLARATION FORMS, ETC)?

travel requirements

COUNTRY:

TAKE VACCINES? WHICH ONES? WHAT DO YOU NEED TO SHOW
TO PROVE VACCINATION?

DO YOU NEED A NEGATIVE TEST? WHAT KIND (PCR, ANTIGEN,
ETC)? WITHIN WHAT TIME FRAME OF ARRIVAL? DO YOU HAVE
TO RE-TEST AT CERTAIN INTERVAL

WILL THEY TAKE RECOVERY CERTIFICATES? WITHIN WHAT TIME
FRAME OF ARRIVAL?

WHAT ELSE IS REQUIRED (PASSENGER LOCATOR FORMS,
REGISTRATIONS, TRAVEL INSURANCE, APPS, DECLARATION
FORMS, ETC)?

travel requirements

COUNTRY:

TAKE VACCINES? WHICH ONES? WHAT DO YOU NEED TO SHOW
TO PROVE VACCINATION?

DO YOU NEED A NEGATIVE TEST? WHAT KIND (PCR, ANTIGEN,
ETC)? WITHIN WHAT TIME FRAME OF ARRIVAL? DO YOU HAVE
TO RE-TEST AT CERTAIN INTERVAL

WILL THEY TAKE RECOVERY CERTIFICATES? WITHIN WHAT TIME
FRAME OF ARRIVAL?

WHAT ELSE IS REQUIRED (PASSENGER LOCATOR FORMS,
REGISTRATIONS, TRAVEL INSURANCE, APPS, DECLARATION
FORMS, ETC)?

travel requirements

TRANSITING COUNTRY:

DO THEY REQUIRE VACCINE? WHAT KIND? HOW TO PROVE?

DO YOU NEED A NEGATIVE TEST? WHAT KIND (PCR, ANTIGEN, ETC)? WITHIN WHAT TIME FRAME OF TRANSIT?

WILL THEY TAKE RECOVERY CERTIFICATES? WITHIN WHAT TIME FRAME OF TRANSIT?

DO THEY REQUIRE A PASSENGER LOCATOR FORM AND/OR HEALTH DECLARATION/ONLINE ATTESTATION OF HEALTH? (*THI WILL NEED TO BE MONITORED THROUGHOUT TRAVEL AS IT CHANGES FREQUENTLY WITHOUT NOTICE*)

travel requirements

TRANSITING COUNTRY:

DO THEY REQUIRE VACCINE? WHAT KIND? HOW TO PROVE?

DO YOU NEED A NEGATIVE TEST? WHAT KIND (PCR, ANTIGEN, ETC)? WITHIN WHAT TIME FRAME OF TRANSIT?

WILL THEY TAKE RECOVERY CERTIFICATES? WITHIN WHAT TIME FRAME OF TRANSIT?

DO THEY REQUIRE A PASSENGER LOCATOR FORM AND/OR HEALTH DECLARATION/ONLINE ATTESTATION OF HEALTH? (*THI WILL NEED TO BE MONITORED THROUGHOUT TRAVEL AS IT CHANGES FREQUENTLY WITHOUT NOTICE)*

travel requirements

TRANSITING COUNTRY:

DO THEY REQUIRE VACCINE? WHAT KIND? HOW TO PROVE?

DO YOU NEED A NEGATIVE TEST? WHAT KIND (PCR, ANTIGEN, ETC)? WITHIN WHAT TIME FRAME OF TRANSIT?

WILL THEY TAKE RECOVERY CERTIFICATES? WITHIN WHAT TIME FRAME OF TRANSIT?

DO THEY REQUIRE A PASSENGER LOCATOR FORM AND/OR HEALTH DECLARATION/ONLINE ATTESTATION OF HEALTH? (*THI WILL NEED TO BE MONITORED THROUGHOUT TRAVEL AS IT CHANGES FREQUENTLY WITHOUT NOTICE*)

travel requirements

TRANSITING COUNTRY:

DO THEY REQUIRE VACCINE? WHAT KIND? HOW TO PROVE?

DO YOU NEED A NEGATIVE TEST? WHAT KIND (PCR, ANTIGEN, ETC)? WITHIN WHAT TIME FRAME OF TRANSIT?

WILL THEY TAKE RECOVERY CERTIFICATES? WITHIN WHAT TIME FRAME OF TRANSIT?

DO THEY REQUIRE A PASSENGER LOCATOR FORM AND/OR HEALTH DECLARATION/ONLINE ATTESTATION OF HEALTH? (*THI WILL NEED TO BE MONITORED THROUGHOUT TRAVEL AS IT CHANGES FREQUENTLY WITHOUT NOTICE)*

MY NOTES

MY NOTES

MY NOTES

travel budget

DESTINATION: **DURATION OF STAY:**

	ESTIMATED:	ACTUAL:
AIRFARE		
LODGING		
TRANSPORTATION *TO/FROM AIRPORT; TO/FROM LODGING; TO/FROM ACTIVITIES; RETURNING HOME*		
GASOLINE/PETROL		
FOOD *INCLUDE RESTAURANTS, COFFEE/SNACKS; BAR; GROCERIES*		
ACTIVITIES *SHOWS, THEME PARKS/ZOOS, MUSEUMS, PARKS, ADVENTURE, SIGHTSEEING, ETC.*		
PERSONAL CARE *SPAS, POOL, CLASSES, GYM*		
SHOPPING/SOUVENIRS		
CASH *TAXIS, FOOD STANDS, TIPS, SMALL ITEMS, OR IF CREDIT CARDS ARE NOT READILY ACCEPTED EVERYWHERE.*		
OTHER		

travel budget

OTHER ITEMS/WORKSPACE

	ESTIMATED:	ACTUAL:

to do list

DATE	TO DO:	
3/20	reserve the activities	✓
		☐
		☐
		☐
		☐
		☐
		☐
		☐
		☐
		☐
		☐
		☐
		☐
		☐

to do list

DATE   TO DO:

_____   _____   ✓

_____   _____   ☐

_____   _____   ☐

_____   _____   ☐

_____   _____   ☐

_____   _____   ☐

_____   _____   ☐

_____   _____   ☐

_____   _____   ☐

_____   _____   ☐

_____   _____   ☐

_____   _____   ☐

_____   _____   ☐

_____   _____   ☐

MY NOTES

MY NOTES

MY NOTES

MY NOTES

MY NOTES

Itinerary Design

Before You Make Any Reservations or Purchase Any Tickets...

Create an Itinerary Rough Draft

Once you've chosen your destination(s) and picked when you will be going, the next step is creating a rough draft of your itinerary.

Why are you not buying anything yet? Because your rough draft may highlight something you want to change, change the days/times you want to be there, or could even change the arrival airport or hotel location so it's closer to the activities you are most interested. It's best not to reserve a thing until you know exactly what you want to do.

Start by making a list of all the things you want to see and experiences. Ideally you would have done this in the research section above (worksheets provided above).

Here are a few of our favorite places to get ideas for what to see and do:

Airbnb experiences - AirBnB.com (scroll down to Discover Experiences section)

We always recommend at least one (ideally a couple) AirBnB experiences on every vacation, **typically at the beginning of your vacation**. These experiences are created and led by locals and usually highlight the main characteristics or customs of a city.

For instance, in Tokyo you can learn the art of making Japanese Mochi and go on a Sake tour with a master sommelier. In Italy, you can learn to make homemade pasta with a local grandmother. In Barcelona, you can design and make your own espadrille sandals. There are hundreds of options all over the world.

There are three reasons to include at least one of these in your next vacation:

- **Experience** - Because they are led by locals, they can offer a depth of experience most tourists don't have access to. Whether it is showing you local hot spots, favorite cultural experiences, or teaching you local cuisine, you will gain a much deeper understanding of the place, people, and culture.
- **Inspiration** - We always recommend you schedule these experiences at the beginning of your trip as they tend to always lead to new friends and new ideas you may want to incorporate into the rest of your trip.
- **Value** - These are usually somewhat inexpensive but incredibly rich in experience, making them a great value.

Other places to research potential things to see and do are YouTube, TripAdvisor, and Google blogs and idea websites.

When designing your itinerary, consider the following:

- Is your desired activity open? Many countries close attractions and stores on Sundays and others may do so for country specific holidays or festivals. There are also constantly changing closures due to COVID. Know what is open and what may be closed while there.
- Do they have siestas or other reasons to close mid-day? This will affect the timing of your plans each day to accommodate these closures.
- Is the activity or place available to the public when you will be there? Double-check to make sure places and activities are not under construction or otherwise unavailable to you.
- What is the time zone compared to where you are coming from? Consider your acclimation to the time when planning your activities. Will you likely need to sleep in? Or will you be up super early? Plan early morning activities on days you know you'll be ok waking up early.

Keep scheduled activities to 1-2 per day

Any more than that and you might overbook yourself and be too exhausted for impromptu opportunities. *Leave plenty of free time to explore as you desire or as the whim strikes.*

As you finalize your itinerary, consider the following:

- **Is your lodging choice close to or easily accessible from the activities you want to do?** Can you easily get back and forth or should you move to a different neighborhood?
- **Are there other airports nearby that might be cheaper to fly into but can easily be added to your plan?**
- **Are the activities open and available the days you are wanting to go?**
- **Can you make reservations and/or buy tickets for everything you want to do?** Or, at least know how to get in if you can't. This is important due to limited capacities and other pandemic restrictions – things just aren't as openly available as usual.
- **Have you over-booked yourself?** Is there plenty of time for being spontaneous and relaxing?
- **Do not have ANYTHING booked on your travel days**. The airports are taking much longer than before, and you won't want to stress about missing a reservation. Let your travel days be only about travel (and checking in to your hotel).
- **Check your timing** – have you given yourself enough time to get to/from each activity? Do you have enough time to change/get ready for the next thing? Are you going to need a nap first?

Now that you know EXACTLY what you want and that it's available, you can begin buying and booking everything.

Tips for Booking Flights

Currently, the best and cheapest online booking engine is **Google Flights**. We've tested several, including Travel Industry only options, and Google Flights beats everyone else 99% of the time.

We've spent quite a long time detailing exactly how to use Google Flights and all the tricks for getter better airfare on our YouTube channel - https://www.youtube.com/c/CraftedTravelCompany – so we won't belabor the point here. Please visit that channel for our top tips for booking flights.

Tips for Choosing and Booking Your Lodging

In every city there are a multitude of lodging options today, from hotels and resorts, to camping and glamping, to hostels, and vacation rentals (including boats, castles, and lighthouses).

This is great because you can experience some pretty amazing things.But it's also a pain because it can make it hard to choose the right option for your specific vacation wants and needs.

There are few tricks to 1) finding what's available and 2) choosing which one is best. As we have with flights, we've created quite a few walk-through videos on choosing lodging and finding the best prices on our YouTube channel. But here are a few of the top tips and resource links to help you get started.

Prior to researching options, you need to:
- Decide what neighborhood or area you want to stay in. You've completed your itinerary rough draft at this point, so you should know which neighborhoods work best for the activities and experiences you'd like to have. But in addition to location, you also need to choose neighborhoods based on budget, safety, and transportation options.
- Decide what level and type of lodging you desire (is a youth hostel fine or do you want a luxury resort? A home rental? A bed and breakfast? Camping? Or something unique such as a castle, boat, or igloo?).
- What are you willing to spend on your lodging each night (based on your budget)?

Once you know these answers, there are three main areas we recommend you being your research:

YouTube – a great resource for ideas and walk-throughs of specific hotels and neighborhoods.

TripAdvisor – This is especially helpful if you'd like to find a hotel/resort with the top ratings in a specific area. TripAdvisor has a ranking of the top hotels based on reviews that can help you pinpoint a few options that will work well for your needs.

For hotels and resorts:

GoogleHotels - https://www.google.com/travel/hotels
Trivago - https://www.trivago.com/
The hotel websites directly (once you've pinpointed a few potential options)

For private home rental:

AirBnB - https://www.airbnb.com/
VRBO - https://www.vrbo.com/
Luxury Retreats - http://luxuryretreats.villas/
GoogleHotels - https://www.google.com/travel/hotels (see bottom icon on left-hand menu)

For camping/glamping:

GlampingHub - https://glampinghub.com/
RV Share (USA) - https://rvshare.com/
Indie Campers (Europe) - https://indiecampers.com/
Campanda (worldwide) - https://www.campanda.com/
Recreation.gov (USA) - https://www.recreation.gov/
Camping Info (Europe) - https://www.camping.info/en
AutoEurope Motoromes (Worldwide) - https://www.autoeurope.com/motorhome-rental

Bed and breakfast:

BedandBreakfast (Europe) - https://www.bedandbreakfast.eu/?lang=en
BnBFinder (Worldwide) - https://www.bnbfinder.com/

Hostels:

HostelWorld - https://www.hostelworld.com/

When choosing your lodging, consider:

- Where you will be traveling each day (all over the city or in specific areas) - choose something centrally located to these or with easy transportation back and forth
- Neighborhood - including available restaurants, shops, safety, and convenience
- Lodging ratings & reviews
- Cost per night
- Amenities - does it include free breakfast? parking? Wifi? Does it offer COVID testing for return flight (or flight to next location)?

Book your lodging (preferably with a reputable company)

By this we simply mean booking with an established company, whether one of the websites linked above or the hotel/lodging directly. Try to avoid strange, unknown third party booking engines you've never heard of or who don't seem to have a strong reputation or presence.

This is especially important when traveling abroad to avoid scams and lost reservations. Even something well known, such as Travelocity, creates an extra layer of people to work through if something goes wrong or something needs to be changed. The more direct you can be, the better.

IMPORTANT Buy Travel Insurance...ALWAYS!

Especially now with the pandemic, travel insurance is **more important than ever before**. Travel insurance is vital to help you if you *get sick or hurt, if the country shuts back down and you need to be re-patriated, if your baggage or wallet is lost or stolen, if things are cancelled or delayed, and so much more.* It not only protects your investment (which is significant even for the cheapest vacations) but also your life and health. This is why every embassy from every country recommends all travelers buy insurance. Especially if traveling internationally.

However, not all travel insurance is built the same. Many of the big companies do not cover anything COVID related, so you need to be sure to *read the fine print.* Also, there are many that will not cover simple activities, such as hiking or kayaking. So when deciding be sure to read what's **NOT included** as much as what is.

We've found an insurance company we feel comfortable recommended because it does have some protection for COVID situations as well as covering all the activities (not just the little ones like hiking, but also big things like SCUBA diving, hang gliding, and bungee jumping).

You can learn more about this company with this QR Code.

Transportation

Once you know where and when you will be arriving and where you are going to stay, start planning your transportation to/from the airport as well as to/from your activities.

As always, a great place to start is YouTube. We start here by searching for "city + transportation" or "how to get to x from airport y". Ideally, there will be a video showing you exactly what the airport looks like, where to catch your transportation (whether renting a car, catching a train, or meeting your Uber driver).

Be sure to keep notes on options, good and bad areas, and any safety tips the video shares.

Call the concierge at your hotel:

This step is often overlooked but can be extremely helpful. Your concierge (and even concierge at neighboring or local hotels) can give you a ton of information about the area, transportation options, safety, and so much more.

In addition to learning about the area, also share some of the places you are considering going to get their feedback. They often tell you if something is worth doing or not, the secrets of when to go, and other cool local options and recommendations.

While you are on the phone with your concierge, be sure to also ask:

- Any safety concerns and do they have any tips or recommendations?
- Is wifi readily available or will you need a portable wifi option?
- Is the water safe to drink?
- Can you use credit cards in most places or will you need cash?
- Best way to get to/from the hotel?
- Will you need to rent a car or will public transportation/Uber be fine?
- Do you need/do they suggest having any kind of public transportation passes/tickets?
- Any other activities or recommended spots you should visit?
- Where is the best place to get your negative COVID test for your return home or move to next country?

Make your return COVID Testing arrangements

Don't forget to make arrangement for your return home. At the time of this writing, the US requires a negative COVID test to re-enter the country – whether you are vaccinated or not, citizen or not. So you will need to arrange a time to take your test before returning home.

Here are a few tips for this:

- Know what time frame you need to take it within (oftentimes within 72 hours of your arrival home)
- Know what types of tests are required (PCR, Antigen, etc)
- As your hotel where you can have the test taken or if they offer that service
- Find a place you can make a reservation and make one! There are many walk-in facilities but lines can get crazy long. Don't waste an full vacation day on lines.

Book, reserve, or make reservations for as much as possible

This is most definitely not the time to fly-by-the-seat-of-your-pants.It is vital to reserve, purchase, or make appointments for as much of your planned activities, transportation, lodging, restaurants, COVID testing facilities, and flights as possible.

Due to limited capacities, new restrictions, limited hours and staffing, and so much more, there's a chance you could show up and not be able to get in.

travel details

DESTINATION:	DURATION OF STAY:	
FLIGHT DEPARTURE + CONFIRMATION NUMBERS:		
FLIGHT DEPARTURE + CONFIRMATION NUMBERS:		
LODGING	CONTACT INFORMATION NOTES	CONFIRMATION NUMBER
LODGING	CONTACT INFORMATION NOTES	CONFIRMATION NUMBER
TRANSPORTATION	CONTACT INFORMATION NOTES	CONFIRMATION NUMBER
TRANSPORTATION	CONTACT INFORMATION NOTES	CONFIRMATION NUMBER

travel itinerary

DAY	WHAT TO DO:	CONFIRMATION INFO & NOTES
DAY	WHAT TO DO:	CONFIRMATION INFO & NOTES
DAY	WHAT TO DO:	CONFIRMATION INFO & NOTES
DAY	WHAT TO DO:	CONFIRMATION INFO & NOTES
DAY	WHAT TO DO:	CONFIRMATION INFO & NOTES

NOTES:
....
....
....

travel itinerary

DAY	WHAT TO DO:	CONFIRMATION INFO & NOTES
DAY	WHAT TO DO:	CONFIRMATION INFO & NOTES
DAY	WHAT TO DO:	CONFIRMATION INFO & NOTES
DAY	WHAT TO DO:	CONFIRMATION INFO & NOTES
DAY	WHAT TO DO:	CONFIRMATION INFO & NOTES

NOTES:

travel itinerary

DAY	WHAT TO DO:	CONFIRMATION INFO & NOTES
DAY	WHAT TO DO:	CONFIRMATION INFO & NOTES
DAY	WHAT TO DO:	CONFIRMATION INFO & NOTES
DAY	WHAT TO DO:	CONFIRMATION INFO & NOTES
DAY	WHAT TO DO:	CONFIRMATION INFO & NOTES

NOTES:
....
....
....

travel itinerary

DAY	WHAT TO DO:	CONFIRMATION INFO & NOTES
DAY	WHAT TO DO:	CONFIRMATION INFO & NOTES
DAY	WHAT TO DO:	CONFIRMATION INFO & NOTES
DAY	WHAT TO DO:	CONFIRMATION INFO & NOTES
DAY	WHAT TO DO:	CONFIRMATION INFO & NOTES

NOTES:

Research and plan for the little details. This includes issues such as:

- Coronavirus concerns (covered above)
- What is the local currency and will you need cash or can you use credit cards most places?Is everything contactless?Do you have the proper apps/payment options downloaded on your phone?
- If cash is used, how much will you need daily (be sure to also check if it's recommended to carry only a small amount with you, as is the case in some countries)
- Is WIFI readily available or will you need a mobile hotspot? May be necessary if you are worried about data charges or will need to connect a computer or other devices.
- Any safety advisories, concerns, and recommendations
- Is the water safe to drink?
- What language(s) are spoken and should you learn some key phrases? Some countries have more English speakers than others. Those that don't, it is helpful to know how to say "hello", "thank you", "can you help me", and "excuse me" in the other language.

Print AND BRING copies of everything with you on your trip!

By this we do indeed mean EVERYTHING. Though the idea may seem a bit antiquated, it is always helpful to have hardcopy backups of everything you will need. You never know when your phone might die or you lose data or wifi or something gets stolen and you will need access to these copies.

We recommend bringing copies of:

- Lodging reservations (some countries require this for entry)
- Vaccine Card and/or Negative COVID Tests
- COVID testing reservations (some countries want proof you have a reservation for their testing protocol)
- Boarding passes
- Directions and contact information for all hotels, transportation, activities, places you want to see
- Your passport
- Credit cards
- Activity tickets or entry materials
- Metro passes or other public transportation tickets or passes

logistics checklist

- Transportation to/from airport
- Transportation to/from lodging
- research & obtain passport/visa
- research safety issues & prepare
- What type of payment is generally accepted?
- Where is best to exchange currency?
- What type of transportation options are there?
- Call concierge for recommendations
- Buy travel insurance
- Print copies of all documents
- Leave copy of credit cards/passports with trusted person.
- Check planned activities/sightseeing will be open? (siestas, national holidays, construction...)
- Check for COVID restrictions/requirements
- Time zone concerns (jet lag or will you be up super early at the beginning)
- No more than 1-2 scheduled activities per day
- Call to verify reservations are secured and everyone is expecting your arrival
- Apply for TSA Precheck or Global Entry and make sure the airline has this information
- What will the wifi situation be?
- Will you need a foreign data plan for your phone?
- Download or print directions to all locations (in case you cannot get phone service)
- Download or print transportation schedules if needed (subways, shuttles, etc)
- Will you need a rental car or can you get around via walking, uber, subway, etc?
- Any helpful phrases or words to learn (if traveling to foreign country)?
- Is the water safe to drink?
- Travel Requirements - every country visiting and traveling through (even if just to change planes)

LOGISTICS NOTES

to do list

DATE   TO DO:

_____   _____ ✓

_____   _____ ☐

_____   _____ ☐

_____   _____ ☐

_____   _____ ☐

_____   _____ ☐

_____   _____ ☐

_____   _____ ☐

_____   _____ ☐

_____   _____ ☐

_____   _____ ☐

_____   _____ ☐

_____   _____ ☐

_____   _____ ☐

_____   _____ ☐

packing list

CLOTHING

TOILETRIES

TECHNOLOGY

SAFETY

NOTES

packing list

WEATHER PROTECTION

BOOKS/ENTERTAINMENT

OFFICIAL DOCUMENTS

MONEY OPTIONS

NOTES

Resources

important numbers

Emergency Numbers by Country/Continent:

Australia	000 (112 on cell phone)
Canada	911
Europe	112
Indonesia	118 (Ambulance), 110 (Police)
Japan	119
Mexico	065 (Ambulance), 060 (Police)
New Zealand	111
Singapore	995
United Kingdom	112 999
USA	911

For more countries, visit
https://travel.state.gov/content/dam/students-abroad/pdfs/911_ABROAD.pdf

Embassies by Citizenship:
Australian Embassies:
https://www.dfat.gov.au/about-us/our-locations/missions/our-embassies-and-consulates-overseas
Canadian Embassies:
https://travel.gc.ca/assistance/embassies-consulates
UK Embassies:
https://www.gov.uk/world/embassies
US Embassies:
https://www.usembassy.gov

language phrases
customize to your location

Hello   Bonjour   (bahn-joor)

currency information
customize to your location

Best places to exchange currency:

Cash will be needed for:

tips
Train/subway passes
food carts

How much cash will we need on hand:

Additional notes/reminders:

safety + health information
customize to your location

What has my research said to avoid:

What is the water situation?

Additional notes/reminders:

Metric Conversion Chart

Into Metric   Out of Metric

If you know	Multiply by	To Get	If you know	Multiply by	To Get
Length			**Length**		
inches	2.54	centimeters	millimeters	0.04	inches
foot	30	centimeters	centimeters	0.4	inches
yards	0.91	meters	meters	3.3	feet
miles	1.6	kilometers	kilometers	0.62	miles
Area			**Area**		
sq. inches	6.5	sq. centimeters	sq. centimeters	0.16	sq. inches
sq. feet	0.09	sq. meters	sq. meters	1.2	sq. yards
sq. yards	0.8	sq. meters	sq. kilometers	0.4	sq. miles
sq. miles	2.6	sq. kilometers	hectares	2.47	acres
Mass (Weight)			**Mass (Weight)**		
ounces	28	grams	grams	0.035	ounces
pounds	0.45	kilograms	kilograms	2.2	pounds
short ton	0.9	metric ton	metric tons	1.1	short tons
Volume			**Volume**		
teaspoons	5	milliliters	milliliters	0.03	fluid ounces
tablespoons	15	milliliters	liters	2.1	pints
fluid ounces	30	milliliters	liters	1.06	quarts
cups	0.24	liters	liters	0.26	gallons
pints	0.47	liters	cubic meters	35	cubic feet
quarts	0.95	liters	cubic meters	1.3	cubic yards
gallons	3.8	liters			
cubic feet	0.03	cubic meters			
cubic yards	0.76	cubic meters			
Temperature			**Temperature**		
Fahrenheit	Subtract 32, then multiply by 5/9ths to get	Celsius	Celsius	Multiply by 9/5ths, then add 32 to get	Fahrenheit

Journal

MEMORIES

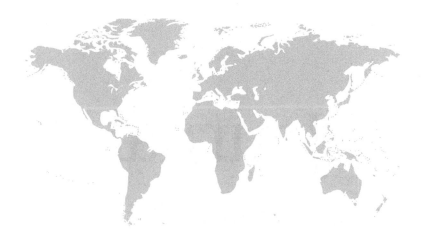

DATE _____

Today I went:

I met:

I had this happen:

But the most memorable thing was:

MEMORIES

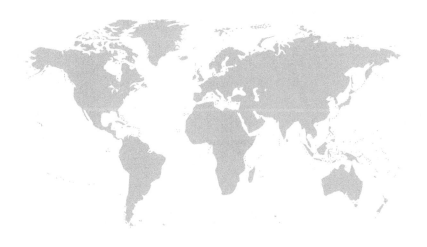

DATE _____

Today I went:
_____
_____

I met:
_____
_____

I had this happen:
_____
_____
_____
_____

But the most memorable thing was:
_____
_____
_____
_____
_____
_____
_____
_____
_____
_____

MEMORIES

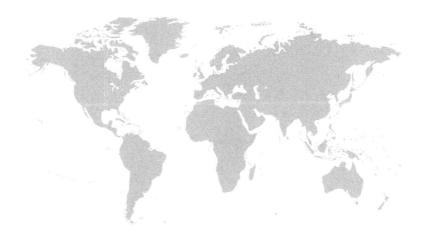

DATE _____

Today I went:
_____
_____

I met:
_____
_____

I had this happen:
_____
_____
_____

But the most memorable thing was:
_____
_____
_____
_____
_____
_____
_____
_____
_____

MEMORIES

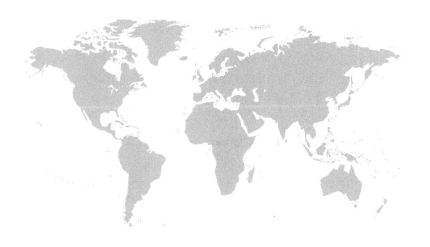

DATE _____

Today I went:
_____
_____
_____

I met:
_____
_____
_____

I had this happen:
_____
_____
_____
_____

But the most memorable thing was:
_____
_____
_____
_____
_____
_____
_____
_____
_____
_____
_____

MEMORIES

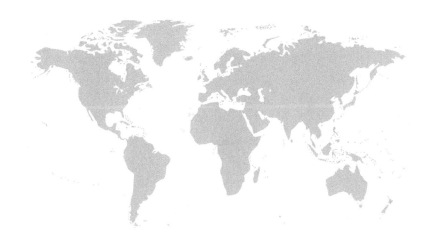

DATE _____

Today I went:
_____
_____

I met:
_____
_____

I had this happen:
_____
_____
_____
_____

But the most memorable thing was:
_____
_____
_____
_____
_____
_____
_____
_____
_____
_____
_____

MEMORIES

DATE _____

Today I went:
_____
_____
_____

I met:
_____
_____
_____

I had this happen:
_____
_____
_____
_____
_____

But the most memorable thing was:
_____
_____
_____
_____
_____
_____
_____
_____
_____
_____
_____
_____

MEMORIES

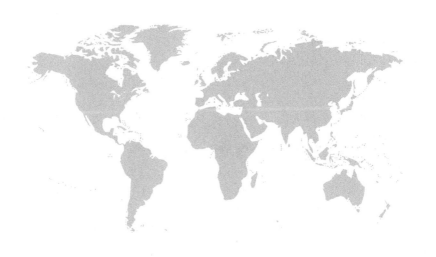

DATE _____

Today I went:

I met:

I had this happen:

But the most memorable thing was:

MEMORIES

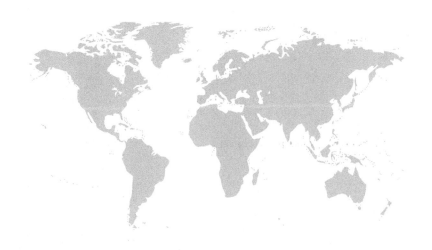

DATE _____

Today I went:
_____
_____

I met:
_____
_____

I had this happen:
_____
_____
_____

But the most memorable thing was:
_____
_____
_____
_____
_____
_____
_____
_____
_____

MEMORIES

DATE _____

Today I went:

I met:

I had this happen:

But the most memorable thing was:

MEMORIES

DATE _____

Today I went:
_____
_____
_____

I met:
_____
_____

I had this happen:
_____
_____
_____
_____

But the most memorable thing was:
_____
_____
_____
_____
_____
_____
_____
_____
_____
_____

MEMORIES

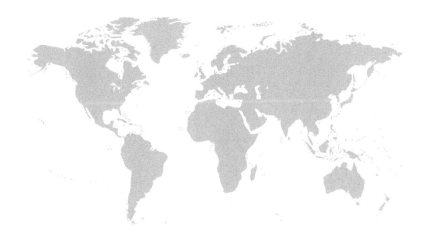

DATE _____

Today I went:
_____
_____

I met:
_____
_____

I had this happen:
_____
_____
_____
_____

But the most memorable thing was:
_____
_____
_____
_____
_____
_____
_____
_____
_____
_____
_____

MEMORIES

DATE _____

Today I went:

I met:

I had this happen:

But the most memorable thing was:

MEMORIES

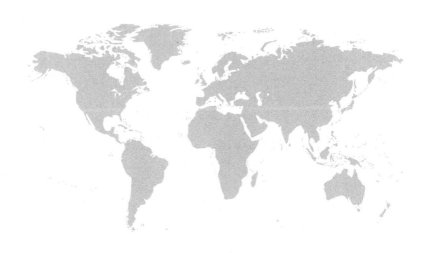

DATE _____

Today I went:

I met:

I had this happen:

But the most memorable thing was:

MEMORIES

DATE _____

Today I went:

_____

_____

I met:

_____

_____

I had this happen:

_____

_____

_____

But the most memorable thing was:

_____

_____

_____

_____

_____

_____

_____

_____

_____

_____

MEMORIES

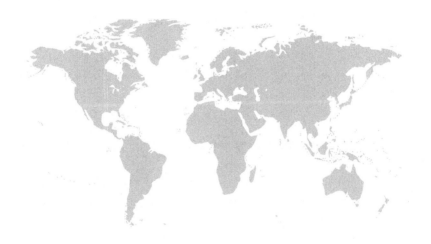

DATE _____

Today I went:

_____
_____

I met:

_____
_____

I had this happen:

_____
_____
_____

But the most memorable thing was:

_____
_____
_____
_____
_____
_____
_____
_____
_____

MEMORIES

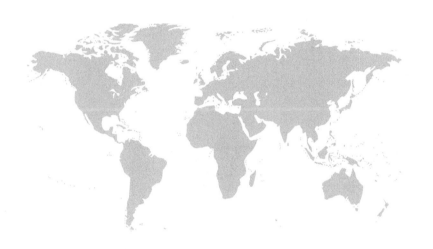

DATE _____

Today I went:

_____
_____

I met:

_____
_____

I had this happen:

_____
_____
_____

But the most memorable thing was:

_____
_____
_____
_____
_____
_____
_____
_____
_____

MEMORIES

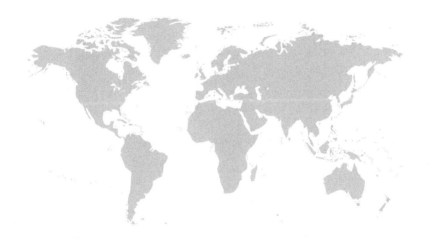

DATE _____

Today I went:

_____

_____

I met:

_____

_____

I had this happen:

_____

_____

_____

But the most memorable thing was:

_____

_____

_____

_____

_____

_____

_____

_____

MEMORIES

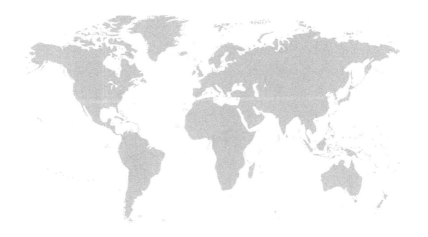

DATE _____

Today I went:

I met:

I had this happen:

But the most memorable thing was:

MEMORIES

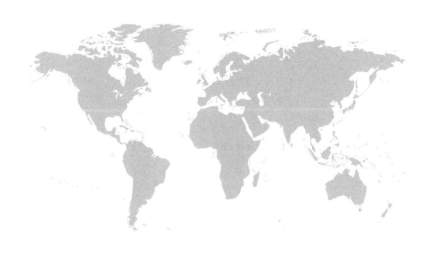

DATE _____

Today I went:

I met:

I had this happen:

But the most memorable thing was:

MEMORIES

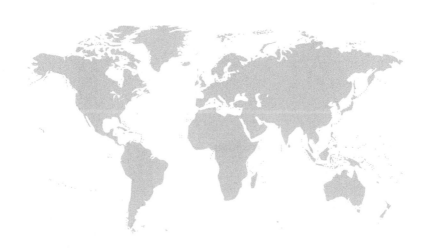

DATE _____

Today I went:

_____

_____

I met:

_____

_____

I had this happen:

_____

_____

_____

_____

But the most memorable thing was:

_____

_____

_____

_____

_____

_____

_____

_____

_____

MEMORIES

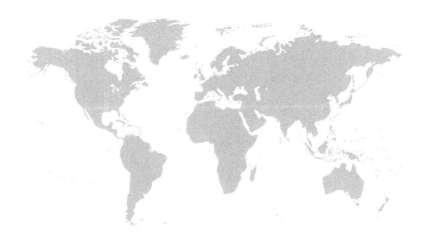

DATE _____

Today I went:
_____
_____

I met:
_____
_____
_____

I had this happen:
_____
_____
_____
_____

But the most memorable thing was:
_____
_____
_____
_____
_____
_____
_____
_____
_____
_____

MEMORIES

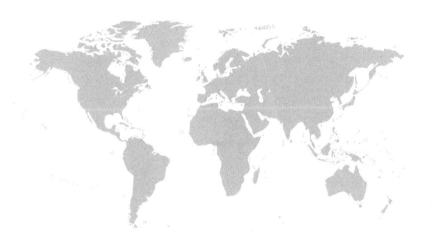

DATE _____

Today I went:
_____
_____

I met:
_____
_____

I had this happen:
_____
_____
_____

But the most memorable thing was:
_____
_____
_____
_____
_____
_____
_____
_____
_____
_____
_____

MEMORIES

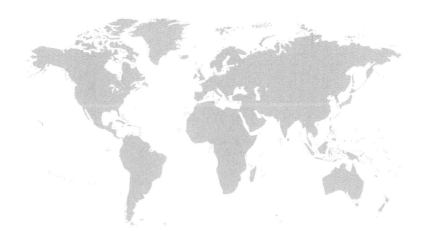

DATE _____

Today I went:
_____
_____

I met:
_____
_____

I had this happen:
_____
_____
_____

But the most memorable thing was:
_____
_____
_____
_____
_____
_____
_____
_____
_____

MEMORIES

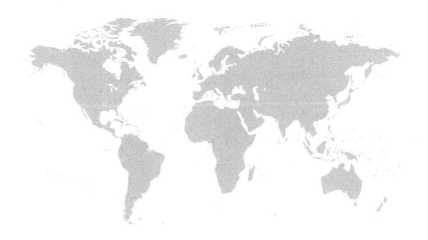

DATE _____

Today I went:

I met:

I had this happen:

But the most memorable thing was:

MEMORIES

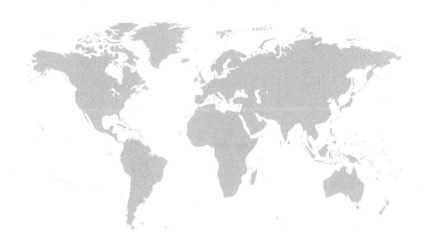

DATE _____

Today I went:

I met:

I had this happen:

But the most memorable thing was:

MEMORIES

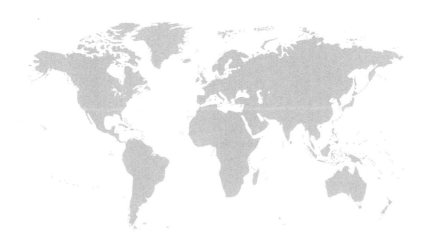

DATE _____

Today I went:

_____
_____

I met:

_____
_____

I had this happen:

_____
_____
_____
_____

But the most memorable thing was:

_____
_____
_____
_____
_____
_____
_____
_____
_____
_____

MEMORIES

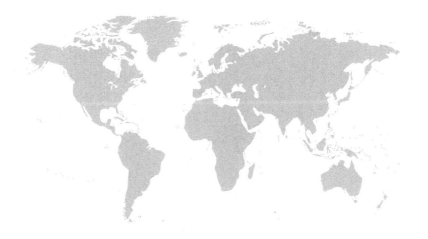

DATE _____

Today I went:
_____
_____

I met:
_____
_____

I had this happen:
_____
_____
_____

But the most memorable thing was:
_____
_____
_____
_____
_____
_____
_____
_____
_____

MEMORIES

DATE _____

Today I went:

_____
_____

I met:

_____
_____

I had this happen:

_____
_____
_____
_____

But the most memorable thing was:

_____
_____
_____
_____
_____
_____
_____
_____
_____
_____
_____
_____

MEMORIES

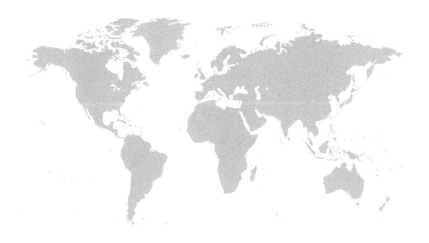

DATE _____

Today I went:
....
....

I met:
....
....

I had this happen:
....
....
....
....

But the most memorable thing was:
....
....
....
....
....
....
....
....
....
....

MEMORIES

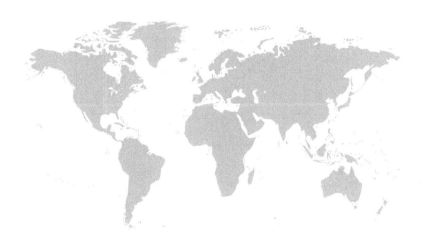

DATE _____

Today I went:

I met:

I had this happen:

But the most memorable thing was:

Thank you for purchasing this book! We appreciate your patronage.

If you have found this information helpful, would you please consider leaving a review on Amazon? This will help us reach more people so their vacations will run more smoothly as well.

Thank you!

Made in the USA
Las Vegas, NV
08 November 2021

34031462R00085